JGOOT ADVENTURE

ULTIMATE GUIDE TO BUDGET-FRIENDLY ESCAPES

Contents

Introduction

Welcome to the exciting world of budget-friendly travel! In this comprehensive guide, we invite you to embark on a thrilling journey of exploration and discovery without breaking the bank. Whether you're a seasoned globetrotter or a novice adventurer, this book is your key to unlocking a world of affordable travel possibilities.

At JGOOT (Just Get Out of Town), we believe that travel should be accessible to everyone, regardless of their budget. We understand the desire to escape the routine, experience new cultures, and create lifelong memories. That's why we've curated this ultimate guide, packed with invaluable tips, insider secrets, and handpicked destinations that will inspire and empower you to explore the world on a budget.

Inside these pages, you'll find a treasure trove of practical advice to help you maximize your travel savings without compromising on the quality of your experiences. We'll share our tried-and-true strategies for scoring the best deals on flights, accommodations, and activities. From lesser-known travel hacks to savvy budgeting techniques, we've got you covered, ensuring that every dollar you spend goes a long way towards creating unforgettable adventures.

So, get ready to unleash your wanderlust and embark on a journey of a lifetime. With the "JGOOT Adventure: Ultimate Guide to Budget-Friendly Escapes" as your companion, you'll be equipped with the knowledge, resources, and inspiration to make your travel dreams a reality, all while keeping your wallet happy. Let's dive in and discover the world together, one affordable adventure at a time!

BUDGET TRAVEL VS LUXURY TRAVEL

What Is Budget Travel?

Budget travel is a style of travel where people go for more cost-effective options and consciously manage their budget throughout their travel. You can get more affordable alternatives for transportation, accommodation, hotels, and food while still aiming to have a meaningful and enjoyable time. If you are taking an adventure trip or a relaxing trip, make sure you are counting all the things while planning!

Make good and right use of your resources and find value in every aspect of the trip. It does not mean that you need to deteriorate the quality of your experiences, but be flexible and mindful of spending your money.
It can take various forms which depend on your personal preferences and travel goals. So, it can involve staying at budget hostels, and guesthouses or taking public transport or budget airlines and opting for local street food or affordable dining options.

Advantages

- The trip becomes much more affordable.

- With fewer financial constraints, budget travelers get the freedom to adjust their itineraries and go for immediate adventures whenever they want.

- People can go for authentic experiences with more budget-friendly options, you can find more of the hidden gems and lesser-known destinations that luxury travelers may overlook during their trip.

- Budget travel motivates people to be more resourceful, and self-reliant in finding affordable solutions and navigating unfamiliar destinations.

Disadvantages

- It takes a lot of research in advance to find the best deals, budget-friendly activities, and reliable hotels.

- You have to be particular with your dates to find the right deals and best discounts for your journey.

- The comfort level in the hotels and accommodations would not be the same.

- There are likely to be more crowds in the cheaper areas and non-luxurious tourist attractions.

- Budget travel will come with more compromises like longer travel times, limited dining options, and less convenient schedules.

What Is Luxury Travel?

It is characterized by indulgence, comfort, and exceptional experiences on your holiday. When you are here to relax, you seek the highest level of quality, personalized services, and amenities throughout the travel journey. The luxury travel prioritizes the premium accommodations, fine dining, and curated activities that provide a great level of comfort.

Advantages

- You get luxurious modes of transportation, which include business class flights, cruises, or your personal vehicles.

- Stay at the premium hotels and luxury resorts, which provide exquisite amenities and great service for the people.

- They also have access to exclusive activities which can also include private tours, VIP access to tourist attractions, and special events.

- Here, more focus is on the personalized service whereby you get a dedicated staff, private guides, and customized itineraries.

Disadvantages

- Luxury travel comes with a high price tag.

- It can also involve a great level of planning and fixed reservations and there is no room for last-minute changes.

- It lacks cultural immersion for the people because it can create a "bubble" for the travelers. It isolates them from the local people and takes them away from the culture.

- There are higher expectations of being perfect and having flawless services.

Budget Travel vs Luxury Travel

1. Prioritize experiences

One of the best ways to find the middle ground is by determining the experiences that have the utmost importance to you. You need to allocate a proper budget to splurge on activities or attractions that hold great value to you.

Also, you need to adopt a more budget-conscious approach for other aspects of your trips that are not so important.

So, you should be in charge of taking care of what you want during the trip. Do not miss the iconic landmarks and main attractions while planning your holiday.

2. Research and find discounts

You should know how to make the best out of the discounts and deals to make your trips filled with luxury. There are many luxurious accommodations, airlines and operators that offer promotions or off-peak prices, which helps you have the best out of your trip.

Make use of the several online platforms that help you get the best discounts. Additionally, you need to consider these great deals to have the best time during the holiday.

Also, you need to take the right moves before you book anything because bargaining can really change the game. All you need to do is go mindfully and see how you can talk to others.

3. Mix your accommodations

You can even blend your accommodations by combining the budget-friendly options with occasional splurges. One of the best travel cost-savings ideas is to use overnight transportation like sleeper trains and buses.

Make sure you are choosing budget hotels or guesthouse solutions. It helps you have a good deal for your staying purpose and experience more communal travel environment. But, make sure you have the necessities in the home to have a good time.

You can also treat yourself to a luxurious resort, or a boutique hotel for a few nights to experience indulgence and relaxation. These can add a touch of luxury to your trip and help you enjoy it even more.

4. Immerse in local culture

Immersing yourself in the local culture while traveling is a transformative experience that always makes you connect more with the destination. You can get to know more about the local culture, norms, and traditions.

You can talk and interact more with the locals during your trip. Also, learning a few things about them can help you have an engaging time mixed with a lot of fun. It is also a way to show some respect for the locals.

This is how you can have authentic insights into the locations without incurring big bucks and expenses. And, that's where the adventure entails your journey.

5. Balance the dining choices

You should know about this balance of your dining experiences which can be done in the budget as well. It is a great idea to enjoy the local food from the stalls and enjoy the vibe over there.

Before the trip, you can also search for some restaurants that can be under your expenses and offer quality food. Many travel reviews and locals can help you find places like these to enjoy your meals.

Also, you can go grocery shopping if you have a kitchen in your apartment. This is how you can make the best out of your journey.

6. Make way for different transportation modes

It helps a lot when you look for transportation options that makes a balance between cost and comfort. There are budget friendly options for taking the transportation, like public transports or shared rides.

But, longer journeys cannot be compromised like this and needs real comfort. So, you need to make the right choice according to your own journey.

7. Make use of local suggestions

Seeking suggestions and recommendations from the locals or fellow travelers would have been the best! It is one of the best ideas to cut your costs with the new things.

Locals and fellow travelers can provide valuable insights into hidden gems and affordable luxury experiences. You will likely end up with many local tips that allow your experience to be unique.

The Allure of Luxury Travel

THE ART OF LUXURY TRAVEL ON A BUDGET

The Allure of Luxury Travel

1. Plan Strategically: Timing is Everything

The foundation of affordable luxury travel lies in strategic planning:

a. Off-Peak Travel
Timing can make all the difference. Luxury accommodations and flights are often significantly cheaper during the off-peak season. Research destinations with shoulder or off-peak seasons and plan your trip accordingly. You'll enjoy fewer crowds and lower prices.

b. Midweek Magic
Traveling midweek can yield substantial savings. Hotels and airlines often offer better rates for stays and flights on Tuesdays and Wednesdays.

c. Flexible Dates
Use flexible date search tools when booking flights. This allows you to find the best deals around your preferred travel dates.

2. Hunt for Deals and Discounts

Luxury doesn't have to mean luxury prices. Seeking out deals and discounts is a crucial part of mastering affordable luxury:

a. Join Travel Reward Programs
Loyalty programs offered by airlines and hotel chains can provide significant discounts and exclusive offers. Sign up and start accumulating points for future luxury adventures.

b. Use Travel Booking Websites

Websites like Kayak, Skyscanner, and Expedia allow you to compare prices across various platforms, ensuring you get the best deals on flights and accommodations.

c. Set Fare Alerts

Use fare alert services to monitor airfare fluctuations. This way, you can snatch up deals as soon as they become available.

3. Opt for Luxury Apartments or Villas

Consider renting a luxury apartment or villa instead of booking a hotel room. This option often provides more space, privacy, and the ability to cook your meals, saving you money on dining out.

4. Embrace the Sharing Economy

Platforms like Airbnb and HomeAway offer a wide range of luxurious accommodation options at competitive prices. Plus, you'll often get the chance to stay in unique properties, from chic city lofts to remote countryside estates.

5. Use Public Transportation

While limousines and private transfers are luxurious, they come at a premium cost. Instead, opt for public transportation or ride-sharing services to get around. Many cities have excellent public transit systems, and ride-sharing apps can be cost-effective alternatives.

6. Dine Smartly

Indulging in fine dining experiences is a significant part of luxury travel, but you don't have to dine at Michelin-starred restaurants every night:

a. Splurge Strategically
Choose one or two special dining experiences during your trip and opt for more budget-friendly options the rest of the time.

b. Explore Local Cuisine
Discover the local food scene by dining at neighborhood eateries, food markets, and street vendors. This not only saves money but also provides a more authentic culinary experience.

7. Take Advantage of Free and Low-Cost Activities

Luxury travel isn't just about where you stay and eat — it's also about what you do:

a. Free Tours and Attractions
Many destinations offer free walking tours, museum days, and public events. Research and plan your itinerary around these cost-free experiences.

b. Enjoy Nature
Nature offers some of the most luxurious experiences. Explore national parks, hike through scenic landscapes, and relax on pristine beaches — often at no cost or for a minimal entrance fee.

8. Consider All-Inclusive Packages

While they may seem expensive upfront, all-inclusive packages often provide excellent value for money. These packages typically include accommodations, meals, drinks, and activities, allowing you to indulge without worrying about additional expenses.

6. Dine Smartly

Indulging in fine dining experiences is a significant part of luxury travel, but you don't have to dine at Michelin-starred restaurants every night:

a. Splurge Strategically
Choose one or two special dining experiences during your trip and opt for more budget-friendly options the rest of the time.

b. Explore Local Cuisine
Discover the local food scene by dining at neighborhood eateries, food markets, and street vendors. This not only saves money but also provides a more authentic culinary experience.

7. Take Advantage of Free and Low-Cost Activities

Luxury travel isn't just about where you stay and eat — it's also about what you do:

a. Free Tours and Attractions
Many destinations offer free walking tours, museum days, and public events. Research and plan your itinerary around these cost-free experiences.

b. Enjoy Nature
Nature offers some of the most luxurious experiences. Explore national parks, hike through scenic landscapes, and relax on pristine beaches — often at no cost or for a minimal entrance fee.

8. Consider All-Inclusive Packages

While they may seem expensive upfront, all-inclusive packages often provide excellent value for money. These packages typically include accommodations, meals, drinks, and activities, allowing you to indulge without worrying about additional expenses.

TOP
DESTINATIONS

PLACES TO VISIT

ASIA

Budget-friendly Asia travel destinations offer diverse cultures, stunning landscapes, and vibrant cities without overspending.

EUROPE

Lorem ipsum dolor sit amet, consectetur adipiscing elit. Proin bibendum lacinia ante ut pulvinar. Etiam a molestie ipsum.

AFRICA

Lorem ipsum dolor sit amet, consectetur adipiscing elit. Proin bibendum lacinia ante ut pulvinar. Etiam a molestie ipsum.

AMERICA

Lorem ipsum dolor sit amet, consectetur adipiscing elit. Proin bibendum lacinia ante ut pulvinar. Etiam a molestie ipsum.

Asia

Budget-conscious travelers should not ignore the list of cheap Asia travel destinations. Let's explore the top places where you will have the opportunity to explore diverse cultures, stunning landscapes, and vibrant cities without breaking the bank.

Bangkok, Thai Land

When discussing Southeast Asia travel, Thailand stands out as one of the cheap countries in Asia to visit, with a particular focus on its capital, Bangkok. Bangkok boasts a vibrant tapestry of traditions, from lively local markets and stunning gilded temples to rooftop bars and vast contemporary shopping centers. Upon your visit, make sure not to miss out on Wat Pho, Wat Arun, and the Grand Palace. Moreover, the lively streets of Khao San and Chinatown offer cost-free opportunities for immersing yourself in the local way of life. Don't forget to explore Thailand's most delectable street food, all at incredibly affordable prices, for a cheap Asia trip.

Hanoi, Vietnam

What is the cheapest Asian country to visit? Prepare a Vietnam travel itinerary, and you will find the answer. Hanoi, the capital of Vietnam, is among the cheap places to travel in Asia. This is a captivating destination that seamlessly blends historical heritage and rich cultural traditions, featuring distinctive architecture and lush green spaces. When you visit Hanoi, you can explore the radiant Hoan Kiem Lake and the charming The Huc Bridge and pay your respects at the Ho Chi Minh Mausoleum. Hanoi is also renowned for its traditional Old Quarter neighborhoods where travelers can savor traditional delicacies such as pho, banh cuon, and cha ca.

Siem Reap, Cambodia

If you are looking for one of the cheap travel destinations in Asia, consider heading to Siem Reap, where you can explore a myriad of historical, traditional, and cultural facets. Siem Reap serves as the gateway to one of the world's most remarkable wonders, Angkor Wat. This temple has held UNESCO status since 1992 and showcases the pinnacle of Khmer architectural excellence. Furthermore, if you wish to immerse yourself in a blend of ancient atmospheres with a touch of vibrancy, you can explore Angkor Thom Temple, the Siem Reap Night Market, and the Tonle Sap Floating Village. To complete your experience, be sure to sample Khmer cuisine and indulge in a soothing foot massage after a day of exploration.

Goa, India

Travelers who want to experience cheap travel in Asia should not overlook Goa, the smallest state in India but one of the most beloved destinations. Here, you can relish a laid-back lifestyle on beautiful beaches and relax in chilled-out shacks. If you crave a bit of excitement, the buzzing beachside bars, the Saturday Night Market, and the Anjuna flea market are must-visit spots. Additionally, the architectural scenery in Old Goa fascinates many travelers with its crumbling forts, impressive baroque architecture, and whitewashed churches.

Bali, Indonesia

Bali stands out as the perfect destination for those who wish to behold stunning Asian beaches while seeking one of the cheap Asia travel destinations. Bali exudes a serene and picturesque atmosphere with awe-inspiring temples, endless beaches lapped by aquamarine waves, and lush green rice paddies. Moreover, this place possesses a tranquil energy that draws those in search of relaxation, well-being, and inner balance. If you want to enjoy a cheap Asia trip and return feeling healthier and happier in Bali, don't miss out on the unique experiences it offers. These include riding a bike through scenic rice fields, riding the waves on pristine white sandy beaches, visiting Hindu temples, and exploring traditional activities.

Cebu, Philippines

Cebu ranks as the most frequented tourist destination in the Philippines and is also featured on the list of cheap travel destinations in Southeast Asia. Cebu boasts numerous pristine white-sand beaches, picturesque islands, breathtaking waterfalls, thriving marine ecosystems, lush natural landscapes, adventure parks, and a wide array of outdoor activities to cater to every traveler's preferences. For those keen on exploring heritage sites like Fort Santiago and Magellan's Cross, a visit to the heart of Cebu City is a must. If you are seeking an island party atmosphere, Moalboal is the ideal destination, offering diverse diving and snorkeling locations.

Kathmandu, Nepal

For those with an affinity for Buddhism, culture, and majestic natural beauty, a visit to Kathmandu in Nepal, one cheap Asia travel destination, is a must. Make sure to explore the Narayanhiti Palace Museum, the awe-inspiring Durbar Square with magnificent palaces and temples, and the Boudhanath Temple, a center of Tibetan culture rich in Buddhist symbolism. Kathmandu is also the perfect base for various adventures, ranging from treks through the Kathmandu Valley to bungee jumping. To complete a perfect cheap Asia vacation, don't forget to savor the local delicacies in Kathmandu, like "momo," – dumplings filled with options like buffalo, chicken, or vegetables, or "chiya" – a milky tea.

Vientiane, Laos

Laos is renowned as the cheapest country in Southeast Asia to visit, and a journey to Vientiane promises wonderful experiences. It is adorned with colorful colonial architecture and boasts a lively nightlife scene. When you visit Vientiane for an affordable Asia travel adventure, don't miss out on visiting the popular Buddha Park. Take time to admire the Great Stupa, the country's most significant monument, explore the Lao National Museum, or enjoy a leisurely bike ride along the tranquil Mekong River to soak in the fresh air and peaceful scenery. And, of course, don't forget to savor Laos' delectable street food offerings, such as "laap" (a salad with minced meat and spices) and "mok" (steamed fish wrapped in banana leaf).

Yangon, Myanmar

Regarded as the cheapest place in Asia to travel, Yangon, the former capital of Myanmar, boasts a plethora of cultural treasures. While it is most renowned for the towering 300-foot gilded Shwedagon Pagoda, Yangon also offers colossal Buddha statues, serene lakeside parks, and vibrant markets. Despite the ongoing modernization, Yangon retains a strong connection to its historical roots, setting it apart from other countries in Asia. Whether you are in the mood for shopping for unique handicrafts, exploring history at museums like the National Museum, or embarking on a culinary adventure with a fusion of Indian and Burmese flavors from street vendors, Yangon will never disappoint you.

25

Nha Trang, Vietnam

For beach enthusiasts looking to explore tourism in Vietnam, don't overlook Nha Trang, one of the cheapest places to travel in Southeast Asia. This coastal gem, hosting a rich marine ecosystem that is nearly unparalleled, boasts a network of islands, pristine white sandy beaches, and untouched coral reefs. While you visit Nha Trang for swimming, mud baths, snorkeling, and various water activities, you cannot miss indulging in the delectable fresh seafood dishes. Beyond its natural beauty, Nha Trang is filled with distinctive architectural landmarks and culturally significant historical sites, such as Thap Ba Ponagar. As one of the safest places to travel in Southeast Asia, there is no reason not to plan your journey to discover the wonders of Nha Trang.

Phnom Penh, Cambodia

Phnom Penh, the charming capital of Cambodia, is one of the cheap Asia travel destinations. This vibrant city boasts undeniable allure, with bustling markets, a thriving art scene, diverse street food experiences, and remarkable architectural gems. Along the walkable riverfront, you will find the ornate Royal Palace and Silver Pagoda. For a more tranquil experience, visit Wat Botum Park, the National Museum, or the Toul Sleng Genocide Museum to delve deeper into the nation's history and culture.

Kuala Lumpur, Malaysia

For those seeking an affordable Asian travel experience, a visit to Kuala Lumpur is a must. This city, among the cheap Asian places to travel, is known for its diverse culture, cuisine, and architecture, all while offering sensational shopping. Modern skyscrapers stand alongside traditional temples and mosques, and massive malls like Pavilion, Mid-Valley Megamall, and Publika provide iconic shopping experiences. For a more authentic culinary adventure, explore vibrant areas like Chinatown and Bukit Bintang to savor beloved hawker stall dishes and soak in the local atmosphere.

Bishkek, Kyrgyzstan

Bishkek, the capital of Kyrgyzstan, is on the list of cheap Asia travel destinations that blend modern cosmopolitanism with Kyrgyz culture and Soviet-era architecture. Markets like Osh Bazaar offer unique items from the Soviet era, and the Kyrgyz National Opera and Ballet Theatre is a hub for Central Asian art. History enthusiasts can explore the Kyrgyz State History Museum, which showcases the cultural heritage of the Kyrgyz people. Additionally, don't miss the chance to savor traditional cuisine and craft beers when enjoying your cheap travel in Asia.

Almaty, Kazakhstan

If you are searching for one of the cheap Asian vacation destinations, consider Almaty in Kazakhstan, a charming city with pedestrian-friendly streets, cozy wine bars, and charming cafe-filled lanes. Surrounded by snow-capped mountains and lush green spaces, Almaty exudes a European ambiance. Almaty features distinctive Soviet-style architecture, with notable structures like the Hotel Kazakhstan, the Palace of the Republic, Arman Cinema, Republic Square, and the Kazakh State Circus. To escape the city and revel in the natural beauty, head to Big Almaty Lake.

Sri Jayawardenepura Kotte, Sri Lanka

Sri Jayawardenepura Kotte, one of the cheap destinations to travel in Asia, appeals to history and political science enthusiasts. This city combines urban vibes with rural elements like rice paddies and plantations. A trip to Sri Lanka would not be complete without a visit to Viharamahadevi Park, featuring lotus ponds, majestic trees, and a stunning fountain. Explore the Colombo Fort, the central business district with British-style structures, local vendors, and traditional cafes and restaurants serving delicious delicacies. Don't forget to visit the Gangaramaya Temple, a highly revered place of worship.

31

Tbilisi, Georgia

For travelers seeking the cheapest vacation in Asia, Tbilisi, the capital of Georgia, offers a unique blend of natural beauty and rich cultural history. Tbilisi is a fascinating city where you can explore Bronze Age settlements, medieval temples, enduring fortresses with a history of battles, architectural wonders, and museums, all of which reveal Georgian treasures, history, culture, and art. In addition to its historical sites, Tbilisi boasts beautiful waterfalls, serene lakes, and breathtaking city and mountain views.

Yerevan, Armenia

For travelers seeking the cheapest vacation in Asia, Tbilisi, the capital of Georgia, offers a unique blend of natural beauty and rich cultural history. Tbilisi is a fascinating city where you can explore Bronze Age settlements, medieval temples, enduring fortresses with a history of battles, architectural wonders, and museums, all of which reveal Georgian treasures, history, culture, and art. In addition to its historical sites, Tbilisi boasts beautiful waterfalls, serene lakes, and breathtaking city and mountain views.

Dushanbe, Tajikistan

For a perfect Central Asia travel experience and affordable Asian travel, consider planning a visit to Dushanbe, the capital of Tajikistan. Dushanbe has its own unique charm, with grand architecture adorning tree-lined avenues and quirky Soviet-era art embellishing walls. Explore iconic landmarks in the city, such as the Ayni Opera, the Museum of Antiquities, Rudaki Park, and the National Museum. Additionally, a visit to the Ismaili Centre, a cultural center and prayer house for the local Shia Ismaili minority, provides insight into Islamic culture.

Ulaanbaatar, Mongolia

If you have a modest budget and wish to experience the cheapest travel in Asia, consider a visit to Ulaanbaatar, Mongolia – one of the best places to visit in Asia. This young and vibrant city seamlessly blends Soviet and Asian influences, offering a wide range of attractions. Art and culture enthusiasts can explore some of the city's best museums, including the National Museum of Mongolian History and the Zanabazar Museum of Fine Art. To experience serenity and spirituality, a visit to Gandan Monastery will leave you in awe.

Lahore, Pakistan

Lahore stands as a vibrant cultural hub and a testament to the country's rich heritage. It is also known as one of the cheap Asian tourist destinations. Lahore's heart, the Walled City, is a bustling area filled with history and heritage, like the Lahore Fort and the grand Badshahi Mosque. The Walled City also houses the revered Gurdwara, a significant Sikh pilgrimage site. Exploring Lahore's streets is like a journey through time while embracing the city's vibrant present.

Dhaka, Bangladesh

If you are asking, "Where should I travel for cheap vacations?", one of the standout destinations is Dhaka in Bangladesh, known for its rich historical importance and numerous tourist attractions. Tourists flock to the city to visit temples, mosques, churches, and forts renowned for their stunning architectural beauty. Some must-visit destinations in Dhaka include Lalbagh Fort, Ahsan Manzil, or Pink Palace, and the Liberation War Museum. Don't forget to explore the diverse and flavorful Bangladeshi cuisine, known for its rich spices and impressive flavors.

Baku, Azerbaijan

Among the list of the cheapest places in Asia to travel, Baku, the capital of the Republic of Azerbaijan, stands out. This cheap Asia travel destination offers some notable landmarks, including Icheri Sheher (Old City), recognized as one of the endangered world heritages in 2003, and boasts over 50 historical buildings. The Palace of the Shirvanshahs is now a museum housing the tomb, mosque, and Turkish bath, as well as the National Museum of History of Azerbaijan, which features over 300,000 ethnographic and archaeological artifacts.

Tashkent, Uzbekistan

Among the various Asia destinations, Tashkent in Uzbekistan stands as one of the cheapest places in Asia to travel. It seamlessly blends medieval buildings reminiscent of ancient oriental tales with elegant European architecture from the time of Turkestan's governorship. Tashkent tours offer a unique blend of modern cityscapes and timeless history, featuring iconic locations like the Chorsu Bazaar and the awe-inspiring Hazrat Imam complex, providing insights into the city's thriving culture, diverse architecture, and remarkable past.

Europe

Europe has a real mix of something for everyone: romantic weekends away, fast-paced city breaks, lazy holidays on the beach, active adventures in the mountains, and plenty of cheap places to visit in Europe if you're on a budget.

Tirana, Albania

Ten years ago, Albania was rarely on the radar of Brits craving a city break. That's changing fast. Social media feeds showcasing the beauty of Albania's coastal stretches have piqued interest in the destination, and, in turn, many travellers are dipping their toes into the country with a long weekend in the capital. Since emerging from a drowsy communist slumber in the 1990s, the city is alive with colour and curiosity. Learn about Albania's fascinating past at the National History Museum before boutique-hopping and coffee-sipping in upmarket Blloku. Best of all, Tirana offers some of the cheapest rooms in Europe.

Istanbul, Turkey

Europe's only bi-continental city is a feast for the senses. Gold glistens from shop windows in the Grand Bazaar, piles of saffron and heaps of cinnamon scent the Spice Bazaar, and stomachs rumble on tours of the ancient city's tastiest, in-the-know spots. Religions and cultures clash at every corner – marvel at the Blue Mosque before a short walk to the gilded Hagia Sophia, originally a 6th-century church. The pound goes a long way here, so ensure there's space in the suitcase to return with cupboard essentials and fashionable finds. Should you fall in love with the hand-woven carpets and art, shipping may be a necessary expense.

Krakow, Poland

Poland's second city is rich in culture, has a thriving hospitality scene, and is pleasingly easy on the pursestrings. In the lead-up to Christmas, historic squares house charming markets where traders sell punchy, steaming concoctions and festive trinkets. Over summer, the same corners of the city come alive as visitors drink and dine on the cobbles before itinerary ticking their way around with visits to the imposing St Mary's Basilica and trips down the Vistula.

Mostar, Bosnia and Herzegovina

Cut off from the intricate rail network that has served much of Europe for over 25 years, Bosnia and Herzegovina retains a mystique that draws in-the-know travellers over the border from nearby Croatia in growing numbers. The country is home to one of the continent's few remaining Indigenous Muslim populations and is a world away, architecturally, from neighbouring countries known for their beach resorts. Mostar's highlights can be done in a day, but allow two or three, perhaps incorporating a day trip outside the enchanting city, to get under the skin of a destination so many travellers know such little about.

Lisbon, Portugal

If you'd like to plan a trip, several budget airlines fly from London to Lisbon (Ryanair, easyJet, Wizz Air, Tap Air Portugal), and while the pretty Portuguese capital is known for its award-winning restaurants, travellers can still dine out on a dime – a three-course meal averages around £39. On the move, you'll get change from a two-euro coin when buying coffee or a mandatory pastel de nata from Pastéis de Belém. Beer here is the cheapest of any city that came out in the top 10 at around £2.26 (putting London's £6 pints to shame) and a Viva Viagem card can save you up to half off tram journeys.

Athens, Greece

This year's Post Office City Costs Barometer ranked Greece's historical capital as the fourth cheapest city break in Europe. Hotels in Athens are particularly good value, with plenty of small, family-run and boutique bedrooms. According to the survey, two nights at a three-star hotel for two guests average £89 – but super-central One Three One is steps away from Monastiraki Flea Market and goes as low as £52 per night.

Riga, Latvia

According to the Post Office, Riga is one of the cheapest cities in Europe – it came out fifth in the 2023 rankings. Wind your way through the narrow alleyways of the charming Old Town, find €2 samsas for lunch at the central covered market located in converted Zeppelin hangars, watch free live music in Dome Square and see striking architecture such as the House of the Blackheads (€6 entry) and the medieval Swedish Gate. But one of the most underrated ways of seeing Riga is on the water – rent a paddleboard for just €15 on the banks of the Daugava River.

Zagreb, Croatia

According to the Post Office, Riga is one of the cheapest cities in Europe – it came out fifth in the 2023 rankings. Wind your way through the narrow alleyways of the charming Old Town, find €2 samsas for lunch at the central covered market located in converted Zeppelin hangars, watch free live music in Dome Square and see striking architecture such as the House of the Blackheads (€6 entry) and the medieval Swedish Gate. But one of the most underrated ways of seeing Riga is on the water – rent a paddleboard for just €15 on the banks of the Daugava River.

Lille, France

This French city is accessible via Eurostar in just one and a half hours from London, and flights from London can be as cheap at £43. Once you're there, knowing the under-the-radar places to book is key. Mama Shelter Lille is a colourful haven very close to both of the city's main train stations with rooms from £79, and there are a host of locally revered restaurants nearby. Head to Rue des Bouchers for cute bistrot vibes – Chez Brigitte has a lunch menu offering three courses for €29, or visit some of the local markets for stalls and trucks selling mouthwatering dishes and local-inspired cuisine.

Budapest, Hungary

Delve deeper beyond the typical tourist traps and you'll find a host of tucked away spots that are surprisingly affordable. The city has an incredible architectural heritage, so walk through both sides of the city admiring buildings and you may stumble upon some globally revered masterpieces. There are some amazing hotels in Budapest too, with plenty of affordable options.

Klagenfurt, Austria

When return flights from the UK to Klagenfurt are cheaper than a one-way train ticket from London to Birmingham, it seems rude not to (and as far as I'm aware, Birmingham doesn't benefit from an Alpine backdrop and Mediterranean climate). Klagenfurt is one of Austria's most affordable cities to visit (main courses are around €6; the farmers' market on Benediktinerplatz is a great place for local bargains), and its spectacular setting on the eastern bank of Lake Wörthersee makes it one of the most scenic, too. June is the cheapest time to go, before the summer crowds and wild swimmers descend on the waterfront.

Kaunas, Lithuania

Vilnius has long been topping lists of the cheapest places to go on holiday, but Kaunas to the west is even less expensive, and earlier this year was named as one of 2022's European Capitals of Culture for its music, art and theatre. Its yearly CityTelling Festival hosts a wide variety of performances and exhibitions that place the city's Jewish heritage centre stage, and access to most events is free, while four-star hotel rooms are as little as €60 a night. For the best views of the Baltic city, a funicular up Aleksoto Hill will cost just a couple of euros. The best bargain in town? Spurginė's €0.75 spurgos (or doughnuts).

Berat, Albania

Like Puglia's trulli or Chefchaouen's all-blue buildings, Berat's unforgettable white Ottoman houses are totally unique in their collective existence and visual impact. The simple, traditional rooms inside also provide a super-affordable way to stay here, as many are guest-houses or independently-run hotels, such as Hotel Vila Aleksandar or Hotel Mangelemi, both around £35 per night. Head up the steep cobblestoned streets to see the 13th Century Berat Castle (entry is free) and take in the 'town of a thousand windows' from the top.

Brașov, Transylvania, Romania

A cheaper alternative to Bucharest (which is still, by European standards, incredibly good value), Brașov is surrounded by the scenic Carpathian Mountains. A cable car up to the top of Mount Tampa costs just 20 lei (£3.55) for aerial views of the brick-red rooftops, whilst local tour operator Walkabout provide a free walking tour every morning at 10.30am, setting off from the fountain in Piata Sfatului. Pick up local delicacy kürtőskalács (a spit-roasted, sugar-covered 'chimney cake') to maintain your energy levels from the stall nearby.

Sofia, Bulgaria

Not only did Bulgaria take the lead (side by side with Turkey) as cheapest all-round destination in Europe in the Post Office's Holiday Money Report 2022, but the country is also home to some of the world's cheapest ski resorts. Sofia, the capital, is just over 10km away from the Vitosha Mountains which provide impressive winter conditions for snow bunnies and cost a fraction of the price of resorts in France or Italy. Wine and Bulgarian beers are notoriously cheap, and downtown Sofia is known for its high-energy party atmosphere. Entry to clubs is seldom more than €10, with live DJ sets and late-night events at Maze or Culture Beat (which also has a great summer terrace for cocktails).

Izmir, Turkey

Despite the British pound tanking in recent weeks, it has remained strong against the Turkish lira (at time of writing, £1 would buy you ₺21), so travellers to Turkey can get great value for money. On Turkey's Aegean coast, Izmir has resisted the price hikes of Istanbul and tourist traps of Ankara whilst preserving its 8,500-year-old Kemeraltı bazaar and ancient Roman agora. The historic sites and architectural relics coexist with cosmopolitan culture and traditional cuisine – try pide on the pier or baked potatoes with a choice of toppings at Atıştır Café. An hour out of town is Ephesus, an ancient city built by the Greeks and well worth a detour.

Tbilisi, Georgia

Whilst the transcontinental city of Tbilisi is the most expensive place to live in Georgia, by European standards it's exceptionally affordable for holidaymakers. A cascade of new hotels have opened in the last few years, such as the lovely Guest House Lile with double rooms from £21 per night. Foodies should book a table at Barbarestan, a family-run restaurant with authentic recipes and local ingredients, where you can eat for around £40 each – not bad for somewhere given a nod by the crew behind the World's 50 Best Restaurants.

Africa

Africa is mystic; it is wild; it is a sweltering inferno; it is a photographer's paradise, a hunter's Valhalla, an escapist's Utopia. It's what you will, and it withstands all interpretations. It is the last vestige of a dead world or the cradle of a shiny new one. To a lot of people, as to myself, it is just home.

Kigali, Rwanda

Despite having a tragic past, Rwanda has a rich, vibrant culture and a pristine natural scenery worth exploring. Travelers come from far and wide to see Rwanda's extraordinary biodiversity, from the magnificent gorillas at Nyungwe National Park to Burchell's zebras at Akagera National Park. But Kigali, Africa's most inviting city, is an affordable place to visit during summer. History lovers learn about the country's chequered past and its road to recovery at the Kigali Genocide Memorial. And art lovers visit Ivuka Arts Studio Centre to marvel at art pieces from local artists.

Mombasa, Kenya

Kenya is one of the most affordable countries to visit in Africa, with a unique mix of attractions and tourist activities for every kind of traveler. From having a beach holiday to a thrilling adventure in Tsavo East National Park near the historic Mombasa town, Kenya is truly a magical place to visit. Mombasa is an ideal summer vacation spot for its pristine beaches with fine white sand. Some of the best beaches for taking tranquil strolls and diving trips are in Diani and others in Shanzu for an off-the-beaten-road coastal vacation.

Cairo, Egypt

Egypt is famous for its impressive pyramids, ancient pharaoh mummies, and unique architecture. And one of the most budget-friendly locations to stay and explore this summer is Egypt's capital, Cairo. History buffs explore the fascinating Egyptian Museum to discover a massive collection of Pharaonic antiquities, including jewelry and statues. Additionally, tourists have a mind-boggling experience in the Royal Mummies Hall as they marvel at the well-preserved pharaohs who ruled Egypt more than 3,000 years ago. The hall hosts the mummies of King Ramses II, King Tuthmosis III, and Queen Merit Amon, among others.

Livingstone, Zambia

Zambia is a must-visit for its diverse culture, rugged terrain, and riveting backpacking adventures. Livingstone is one of the cheapest vacation spots in Zambia, packed with thrilling and unforgettable outdoor escapades. Also known as the tourist capital of Zambia, Livingstone is home to the magnificent Victoria Falls, one of the largest and most enchanting waterfalls in the world. During the summer, adventurers have an adrenaline-inducing swim as they admire breathtaking scenes in the natural infinity Devil's Pool at the end of the falls.

Dakar, Senegal

Senegal is one of the most-visited destinations in West Africa, especially for its intriguing UNESCO-listed World Heritage Sites in Dakar, such as Ile Goree Island. This island is a stark reminder of the cruelty and brutality of the transatlantic slave trade through the historic House of Slaves. Enclosed by the Atlantic, Dakar evolved from a colonial trading center to a lively city with golden beaches to keep adventurers busy or relaxed for days. Intermediate and expert surfers ride the waves at Ouakam during the summer as learners head to Virage.

Cape Coast, Ghana

Ghana is a cheap vacation spot in Africa worth visiting for its bustling coastal cities, rich but sad slave history, and mouth-watering food scene. Food lovers will enjoy the creative rice dishes by sampling jollof, waakye, and omo tuo rice dishes. On the other hand, history buffs learn about the painful but extensive transatlantic slave history in the historic Cape Coast city. This city is home to the Cape Coast Castle, where guides take tourists through an emotional slave trade journey.

Zanzibar, Tanzania

Budget travelers looking for destinations with gorgeous beaches, a rich culture, and history go to Zanzibar, Tanzania. Nungwi Beach is one of the most lively areas in Zanzibar, where night owls find a variety of entertainment from nearby bars and restaurants. Besides the nightlife, Nungwi Beach boasts spectacular coral reefs worth exploring via diving or snorkeling. Travelers take a break from the stunning beaches by walking through the narrow mazes of streets in Zanzibar's cultural center, Stone Town. While strolling, tourists encounter iconic wooden doors with Indian and Arab styles dating back to the 19th century.

Windhoek, Namibia

Namibia is one of Africa's most interesting places to visit, boasting surreal landscapes with untamed wildernesses and iconic tribes with mind-blowing cultures. These attractions make the top of the list for most travelers as they often overlook Namibia's capital, Windhoek. Nature lovers will love exploring the country's natural beauty at the National Botanic Garden of Namibia in Windhoek, showcasing indigenous flora and fauna in a natural environment. This pleasant garden also hosts about 75 bird species, which include the rosy-faced lovebirds, acacia pied barbet, speckled pigeons, and blue-breasted cordon bleu.

Marrakech, Morocco

Morocco continues to trend as a picture-perfect destination with many UNESCO World Heritage Sites, a charming historical vibe, and beautiful architecture. The best place to experience the unique Morrocan sounds and sights is Jemaa el-Fnaa Square in Marrakech, by having a street food tour and listening to music. A stay in a budget-friendly traditional riad rewards guests with a first-hand glimpse at the splendid Moroccan architecture. In addition to recharging in a tranquil paradise without the Marrakech noise, tourists have access to a dreamy-looking pool with colored tiles and detailed patterns.

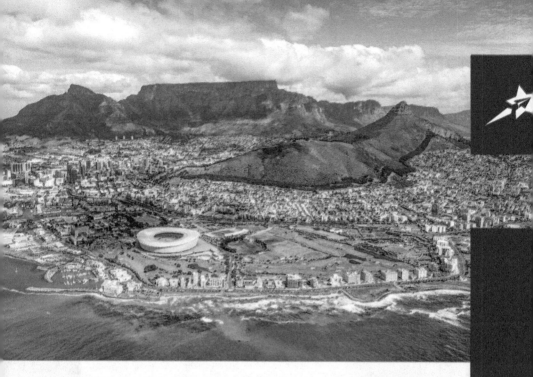

Cape Town, South Africa

South Africa lures travelers with dazzling beaches, exciting outdoor adventures, fantastic culinary delights, and a rich history. Besides the attractions, this country is a budget traveler's favorite vacationing spot with affordable and tailor-made outdoor excursions, especially in Cape Town. In summer, beachgoers enjoy basking in the sun at Camps Bay or seeing the endangered African penguins at the renowned Boulders Beach. Alternatively, nature and photography enthusiasts visit the immaculate Kirstenbosch National Botanical Garden for its diverse floral kingdom and Table Mountain vistas.

68

America

Africa is mystic; it is wild; it is a sweltering inferno; it is a photographer's paradise, a hunter's Valhalla, an escapist's Utopia. It's what you will, and it withstands all interpretations. It is the last vestige of a dead world or the cradle of a shiny new one. To a lot of people, as to myself, it is just home.

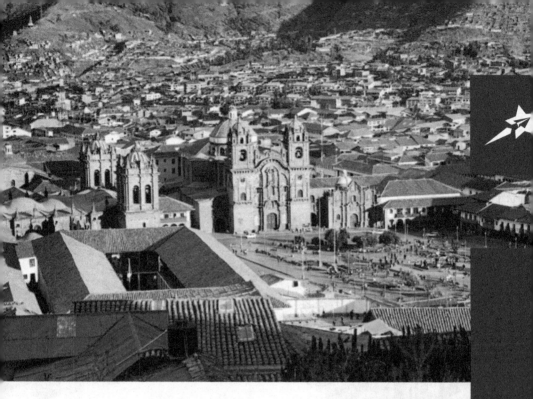

Peru: Cusco and Machu Picchu

This is easily one of the top cheap vacations in South America. Machu Picchu is one of the most famous landmarks in the world, and it's actually very affordable and easy to visit.

For those who don't know, Machu Picchu is a historic Incan city built high in the Andes Mountains in southern Peru. It is a UNESCO World Heritage Site, and Cusco is a nearby city in Peru that acts as the perfect gateway for visiting Machu Picchu.

Ecuador, South America

Quito is the capital city of Ecuador, a country in the north of South America. Flights into Quito from the USA can cost as little as 100 USD. Once you arrive, you'll see why Quito is one of the best cheap and fun places to visit in South America.

Spend your days in the city exploring the historic Old Town, browsing through local markets, relaxing in the parks and gardens, and eating plenty of local food. Quito is conveniently located near lots of other cool places in Ecuador, so it's easy to take day trips from the city.

Bolivia: La Paz, Amazon, Salt Flats

If you're looking for cheap South America vacations, definitely put Bolivia on your list. This interesting and diverse country is full of amazing things to do, and it can all be done on a budget. La Paz is the administrative capital of Bolivia. From La Paz, you can take cheap public transport to any other attractions around the country. Visit the famous Uyuni Salt Flats, hike through the dense Amazon Rainforest, tour a local village, or cycle the famous North Yungas Road cycling trail. Visit the other-worldly Laguna Colorada and see the flamingos, or check out the turquoise waters of Laguna Verde.

Colombia: Cartagena and the beaches

As a cheaper alternative to visiting a tropical Caribbean Island, consider going to Cartagena, Colombia. This port city is a popular place in Colombia, mainly due to its attractive historic Old Town, exciting nightlife, and nearby beaches. After enjoying the city, soak in the surrounding natural beauty and visit the tropical beaches. From the soft white sand to the towering palm trees to the calm, clear ocean, Cartagena is one of the best cheap South America vacation for beach lovers. Enjoy beaches close to the city or take day trips to nearby islands.

Paraguay

Paraguay is an underrated travel destination in South America. Sandwiched between Brazil, Argentina, and Bolivia, it is often overlooked by travelers. However, because it is not very touristy or popular, Paraguay is one of the top cool cheap places to visit in South America.

Paraguay is perfect for nature and adventure lovers. It is home to one of the world's largest wetlands, and also has spectacular waterfalls and lush national parks. Start your journey in Asuncion, the colonial capital of the country.

Patagonia

Paraguay is an underrated travel destination in South America. Sandwiched between Brazil, Argentina, and Bolivia, it is often overlooked by travelers. However, because it is not very touristy or popular, Paraguay is one of the top cool cheap places to visit in South America.

Paraguay is perfect for nature and adventure lovers. It is home to one of the world's largest wetlands, and also has spectacular waterfalls and lush national parks. Start your journey in Asuncion, the colonial capital of the country.

Made in the USA
Las Vegas, NV
28 April 2024

89256297R00046